In the Region of the Heart

In the Region of the Heart

A Collection of Written Fragments

2019

Jack Cain

CODHILL

Codhill Press

Codhill Press books are published by
David Appelbaum
1 Arden Lane
New Paltz NY 12561

First Edition

Cover design by Jack Cain

ISBN 978-1-949933-04-8

Printed in the United States of America

Introduction

Most of these "fragments" were written by me in group poetry sessions that I was facilitating. The sessions were designed to be an exploration of the distinction between material arising from the subconscious mind as opposed to material arising from our ordinary consciousness. This direction came from G.I. Gurdjieff's startling and impertinent statement that our subconscious is our "real" consciousness and our ordinary waking state of consciousness is "fictitious." We would begin in quiet, watch what arose and then write from that. Once everyone was done, we would read the material and speak of the process that each one of us had observed. These exchanges helped us understand that we were much more deeply connected than we realized.

Jack Cain
June 15, 2018

Contents

I dedicate this book

to

Sophia

in all her forms

The Great Ship

The Great Ship is most clearly visible
When 70 people engaged in conversation
Suddenly
Fall silent.

As the quiet gathers strength,
Walls shiver and dissolve.
Food is left uneaten.
And our ascent begins
Through the reciprocating motion
Of each mind and heart
All
Impeccably intent
On duty
And the mission's aim.

Boisterous
Beyond the room,
A summer wind
Shakes through
All the trees
In an exultation of freedom.

Unperturbed
By burgeoning Nature
And with stately grace
The Great Ship proceeds
Upon its charted course
Sustained
By the unearthly sadness
Of a sacred song.

The Cross

(for Nancy)

Using two fingers
Held in front of the body
We are asked to trace the outline
Of a cross
Again and again.
Music from the fingers of the pianist
Helps us all be together
In this movement.
After a time
I see before me images of my mother and father
Who departed this life
Oh so many long years ago.
Their happy presences
Illuminate the meaning –
The intersection point –
Of this cross that we are tracing
In front of the body
Again and again.
Each note on the piano
Touches a resonant chord
Within.
Two worlds
Visible and invisible
Meet
And in us, through us
Are one.

NOVEMBER 3, 2012

There is a damp chill
That comes seeping in
As we sit in the Lake Room
Looking out at the water's surface
That is silvered by the wind.
A group of us has gathered –
Many relative strangers to one another –
Gathered to search together
For meaning and for life.
The world seems too big
And we too small
For this search to ever bear fruit
And yet . . .
And yet . . .
The movement of the silvered surface of the lake
Seems to reflect
The spirit of enquiry that passes
Like a breath
From one person to the next
And on and on
Until there is a sense
That we are here
As one
Just as the silvered lake is one
Each leaf is one
Each breath is one.
The chill is present still
As if there is no firmness yet
In knowing you are me
And I am you.
It has begun to rain.

Solid Ground

The horizon is dark and there is water in every direction. It is not possible to know if I am moving or in which direction. The sky is black. An orchid appears before me. It is violet-hued and attached to a leafy tendril extending up beyond where I can see. I reach out. But it is gone. Once again I am surrounded by water. In its rhythmic sound, my attention is drawn down to the glass floor. I see into enormous watery depths. Queasy, I look away, up, side-to-side, ahead. Much time passes. Then, as if from a time before time, I remember someone. Shadowy and indistinct outlines appear. Who? Desperate, suddenly, I call my name. The bow of the vessel grinds ashore and I step out on solid ground.

Who

Who is this running on the beach?
Breath of the planet on the face
Sand, the base, giving just a little
On impact, and then, spurting up behind:
Legs, arms, pushed in burning circles,
Driving on and on,
Carrying the head
Laughing and bemused
Along the edge of the curling tongue of the sea.
Speak, body . . .
Tell.
Inform this querulous soul –
Who is this running on the beach?

Smile

The morning is a giant's shoulders,
Hunched and massive.
Looking down,
He broods, silent and unmoving.
We feel his weight across our chests,
Within our hearts and lungs and skin.

But from where this unimpeded sound,
Crystalline and sapphire blue?
It enters unperturbed,
Consummately aware,
As it carries messages from home.

Ah, to be one.
Ah, to be what I am.
Dual but one,
Scattered and aligned.
Unrelentingly human.

I smile.

This Moment

This moment
White and crystalline
As we fall toward
The nadir of the year
Implacably.
Letting go of me, and mine
I join, I become
A part of what is cradled
In the winter light.
A joy so quiet it cannot speak
But only shine.

Crust

There is a crust
That has formed over feeling.
It is dark and uneven.
In a certain light
Its dark glimmers have –
Yes – almost a beauty.
It quivers when I say,
"Perhaps it needs to be ripped away."
And it does serve a purpose
Because what is beneath it
Is raw and unprotected
Blind
Unable to see through the opacity.

I did not see her approach.
Suddenly she was there
Standing very near
And smiling.
In her presence I am not
What I was.
Bathed in what she brings
There is a flow of feeling –
A flow that moves
Neither within nor without.
And I am healed.

As the flower opens
There is no doubt or fear.
Only the movement toward fruition.

I know
And I am seen.

Skrying

Rising up through
The reflective surface of still water
In this shallow vessel –
There emerges gently
An intensely blue orchid.
Its color reverberating
Like an infant's cry of joy.

And then not far behind
There rises next
Four horses
Thundering forward
Straining hard to haul
With precipitous intent
A chariot of gold.

As the surface regains its calm
And can once again reflect the depths
There first appears
The tip of his staff
And then very slowly rising up –
An ageless man
With flowing robes and beard.
In his left hand there rests
Ever so gently
The heart-shaped fruit –
The gift of immortality and life.

Looking at the reflective surface
One more time
I see nothing now
But my enquiring face
And all is still.

Cerberus

There is a nether world
That is guarded
Some say
By Cerberus
A creature with three heads
Dogs' heads.
That's all I know
Or have heard.
And yet I sense too
A darkness below
And movement in that darkness.
Three heads on a body.
What is the meaning of head?
I assume they are ferocious, snarling, frothing at the
mouth,
But again I do not know.
The guarding . . . Why?
Why should it be guarded?
To keep in or keep out?
In the bright day I look up
I feel drawn up.
At night too I look up at the stars.
I am suspended.
I am between.
Headless, heartless, incorporeal.
I cannot be.
The terror of coming to know
Who I am.
I must stop
Now
And listen.

Watching

Watching the undeniable descent
Of that which cannot be named
Of that which I cannot call
But that by which I may be called.
And at this moment
Once again
Feeling opens,
Even while the mind remains occupied
By alien forces,
Armies marching through the dusty plain
Bugles sounding loudly,
All the while feeling remains
Quick
And touched by what descends.

Debris

Like the apparent chaos of the forest floor
There is debris scattered everywhere
Inside me.
All of it dead.
The sound of the woodpecker
Pounding away at a dead tree
Comes into me.
I turn
Surprised to be able to see him –
Struck by his intent and his intensity –
His back so straight
Perfectly secure on his feet
Nourishing the life he was given.
Alive.
Finding life in what is dead.
Digging deep.
Gradually I remember it is spring.
I remember how the forsythia shouted at me
As our car rushed by;
Remembered too the articulate green
Of the trees' first growth.
Remember being told I am a vessel
Not a log.
And now I feel
That I am seen.

In Time

Do I have time?
Or does time have me . . . ?
I stand, unsure, at the end
Of day.
There is a subtle movement
Of something unresolved –
A perfume now lost
In the depths of time.
I hear a baby cry.
I see the movement of sunlight
On the water as darkness falls.
Do I have time?
Or does time have me . . . ?
An intimation of greatness
Swirls at my feet.
Grave is the danger now.
Voices clamor at the edge of night,
And the blackbird no longer sings.
Do I have time?
Or does time have me . . . ?
I cannot run
And I cannot stay.
I cannot laugh
And I cannot cry.
I cannot live
And I cannot die.
I can only be
In time.
And great is the glory.
Glory, glory, glory.

No End

He didn't know the room was empty
When he walked in
Because it was dark.
He just stood there
Feeling for the dimensions of what he had walked into.
No light, no sound.
But a sense, gradually,
Of not being entirely alone.
He took a few more steps
As the void absorbed his footfalls
And again he stopped,
Listening for the walls.
But it seemed there were none . . .
Only those thrown up
By a fluttering of doubt.
Then, out of the stillness
A silver chalice was there
Speaking to him of light.
Chest opening
Barely able to encompass
What could not be understood.
"Drink deeply," said the voice
As the darkness descended all around him once again.
Standing still
No sound
He began to drink what can never be contained.
Drinking deeply
Without sound
Without movement
Drinking now and forevermore.
Drinking till no end.

My Heart Is Not Big Enough

My heart is not big enough.
There is a danger that my cup may spill.
I breathe more deeply
So that the light on the water may enter
So that the hymn of grace may be heard
So that the laughter of children may resound.
I see that breath is life
I see that my heart begins to smile
I see that I can laugh with the moon and with the sun.
Rejoice, rejoice, rejoice.
For now I share in a never-ending joy
That is not mine.

Unfettered

Who is this
Who stands before me now
Wise and unfettered in the light?
How could I have ever strayed so far
So that even the memory of this form
Was gone?
Gone. The death knell rings
And rings.
And who in me will hear?
Listen says the light –
Listen with great care –
The window opens wide
And all of Heaven sings
When uncreated light
Is heard.
Listen – listen and you will see
The way is opening now.
Venture, venture forth
Out of regret and into quiet joy.
Yes, yes and yes again
Let the heart resound
And be as one.

The One Who Talks

Where is the one who talks?
I see him standing there.
I see he wants to talk.
But the silent one is present too.
He does not move
He does not speak
His eyes are closed
And I feel irresistibly drawn
Into connection with him.
As if we are linked in kinship
By something I cannot see but feel.
The one who wants to talk
Still wants to talk
But no longer knows the words.
He stands confused – his mouth open and awry.
Suddenly a child runs through,
Laughs and wants to play,
Tugs at their hands
Until both – all three
Begin to enter into life.
And there is sunlight now
Filtering through the trees
And a breeze that washes all our faces clean.

Take Heart

"Take heart"
I heard him say.
But from where does one do that
I wondered.
It feels as though a reach is required.
Something needs to stretch
Extend
Until contact is made.
"Take"
Is also strange in this expression –
Because it's as if I take what is not mine.
Or, if it's mine,
It is impossible to hold,
To keep it fast to me
Because it will not be tied down.
In a flash, it is no longer there,
Much less not "tied down."
So I stop, once again, and
Take heart.
I feel the contact made
And see that I am other, now,
Than how I was.
And in this moment
Hope begins
Anew.

World

Bright and precious,
Trembling on the surface of dark waters
Are the eyes of those assembled here –
Reflecting the movement and exchange of forces
Far beyond the ken of
Any single one of those
Gathered in this vessel –
This alchemist's athanor of harnessed sun –
Fear and boundless love
Narrow bridges
And the call of a distant bell.

Gnome

Yesterday I had the visitation
Of a churlish gnome.
He took hold of me
And shook and shook –
Shook the living daylights
Out of me
Until even the memory of light
Was gone.
Something had to come
From the outside.
Someone had to bring the milk
Of human kindness.
You must have gold
To make gold.
A process was begun.
What is it that is entrusted to my care?
It trembles in the dark.
Someone here must care.

Ground

How strange
That the ground comes to be
Elusive.
Suddenly it is not there
Or it stretches away to the horizon
And the feet do not find it.
Perhaps it is a mistake
To look for it underfoot,
Instead of coming into alignment –
Allowing the spine to relax
Into a network of vertical correspondences.
The sacrum speaks,
And the pelvis begins to allow,
A reverberation begins to move down,
Knees unlock
And gradually the ground is there.
Feet are planted,
"Holy the firm" is found.
And at the core
This gentle reconciling movement –
Something like the color mauve
But quick with love.
And I begin again
To live.

In and Between

Why do I feel that there is a world above me –
Above and beyond me –
Invisible but felt –
And burgeoning with life?
Where in me is the part that has this sense, this feeling
This touch, this intimation of another life,
A richer life than where I think myself to be just now?
Just now.
Just now.
The bell that tolls me back
To here and n ow.
These two worlds
Visible and invisible
Both sensed
Both real
"And neither entirely reliable,"
Someone in me says.
I live in and between.
And yet, and yet . . .
I come back to here and now
And I feel that world above me
And something in me bows down
Deeply
In gratitude
And love.

The Space Before Me Now

This morning as we sat, a rich stillness filled the room –
A feeling of being accompanied
On a journey to the source, to the well.
A feeling of being no longer alone.
And even for a certain time afterwards
Something of that remained.
So I decided to stop
And look at where I am.

The space before me now
Appears to be empty, void, uncluttered
But as I stay with that,
As I continue to observe,
I begin to sense, to feel that this empty space
Quivers at my gaze.
It seems no longer void but vibrates ever so subtly
And there is a sound that is barely heard
A sound that resembles the beating of wings
Many, many wings.
A multitude unmanifest in the world of earthly
perception.

A voice is speaking now:
"Tune the instrument that you have been given."
"Activate the functions you have refused to believe
are there."
"Live what you have been designed to live."

And then words from Krishnamurti arise in me:
"Truth is a pathless land." And
"Sir, you do not realize that the house is on fire."

Quietly now, the fire begins to burn
And I move forward
Knowing and not knowing
Believing and not believing
Alone and not alone.

Walking

I am walking on a street in a very large city.
A part of me assumes I know where I am going.
And a part of me is amused at that assumption.
Two parts of a temporary assemblage
Constructed by intelligent design.
I smile –
And marvel –
At the designer's hand;
Seeing – in a way –
That I am held,
Sustained,
And nurtured by that hand.
A part of the assemblage begins to see:
This is what is meant by Love.
And so the walking is different now
In this very large city.
Walking.
Walking on.

Irreparable Loss

Irreparable loss –
She was facing irreparable loss –
And what was I to say?
Hearing her words then in that moment
Something in me was brought to an abrupt halt.
Recalling it now, my thoughts turn
To the thousands of Mexico's pre-Hispanic paper
    books
Of which only thirteen now remain.
Anger and despair and tears
Seem natural
And yet a quiet voice is saying, "No."
Very softly.
"You must love this movement or you die."
The "No" was hard, but this is harder still.
How can this be?
So I stop – this time not a halt but a stop –
And I allow.
I see I must not think.
Not think but allow.
Something in me stands aside to watch.
Gradually I begin to glimpse
The inexorable movement of all that is.
And I feel in the deepest level of my heart
That to be one with that movement
Is to have wings –
Wings of freedom and of joy.

Lineage

When you meet a stranger's eyes
There can be a clear sense
Of contact and exchange
That is sharpened by its unexpectedness.
Precision and a sense of something very fast
Inform this experience.
When I ask, "From where is the perception of this
    moment taking place?"
It is hard to determine that place.
It feels deeper – even mysterious.
As I now try to be close to that place
I immediately feel a contact
With something that tastes very similar
To when we sit together in meditation.
Something like an atmosphere that I move into
And that penetrates me.

How little I see of the connections between things!
And yet there is a sense of a web or a fabric of these
    very connections.
A fabric that could contain a logic for all that is
And all that happens;
A logic that could provide
Just what is needed for the next step.
A logic that could connect me to a lineage;
A logic that is not imposed
But is very simply there
By virtue of the nature of what is.
I breathe now into that.

Verticality

He said, "Turn inward."
He also said, "Allow."
But when I do there is nothing.
Nothing at all.
So I wonder, "Have I turned?
From where do I turn? What turns?"

Suddenly, something washes over me.
Something like a wave.
I see that I know nothing, nothing at all.
I am no longer stuck but I am adrift.
Alone. Rudderless.

Then I am given a word.
A word comes in.
I don't know where it comes from.
It is not spoken, it just comes in.
The word is "Verticality."
My spine shifts ever so slightly.
A shiver runs up it.
Then it is very still.
There is a world below
There is a world above
And I am between them.
But more miraculous still –
I am I.
I am known and unknown.
There is no then, no now.
There is only this.
Just this.
That is all.

The Bear

Jack: Why have you come to me, bear?
Bear: I have been told to come to you because you have a need.
Jack: A need? What is that need?
Bear: A need to be more fully yourself.
Jack: Can you help me?
Bear: Look into my eyes.
Jack: Yes.
Bear: And now move behind my eyes and look out.
Jack: The world does not look the same.
Bear: Exactly. Can you tell me what the world looks like now?
Jack: There are no words for what I see.
Bear: Exactly. Feel the mass of the body.
Jack: I feel its weight, its bulk and its power.
Bear: Good. Here is a piece of honeycomb. Taste it.
Jack: Mmm . . .
Bear: Repeat this mantra: X X X. But tell no one these words. They are for you alone. Otherwise their power is lost.

The Dwarf

As Zarathustra climbed the mountain
The dwarf who was the spirit of gravity
Jumped off his back
And suddenly Zarathustra was full of light.

Ah, how strongly I feel the presence of that dwarf this morning!
As if he were standing proud within every cell of my body.
At my repeated pleas for respite
He offers nothing but a loud guffaw.
"You have no idea how to find the key," he taunts.
"No idea at all."
"The key?" I say to myself. "There's a key?"
Reading my thoughts he says,
"Of course there's a key – a golden key, in fact."

As I walk through the forest of pines along the lake
I hear their soft voices brought with the morning's first light.
I pause, stopping to listen more carefully
To what their voices say.
"We are born of the moment." I hear them say.
"There is no gravity here in what gives our voices life."
The dwarf frowns – clearly annoyed.
"One clue too many," I hear him grumble.
Stopped in my tracks –
My forward momentum slowed –
I look up.
Beyond the branches the sky is blue.
I enter into its intensity
Carrying in my heart an unspoken need
A message is received in response.
"The voices you have heard are inside you.
You can allow their quality to pervade you –

Pervade every cell."

I turn the golden key
And watch the dwarf trudging away,
Grumbling.

Humbly

Sparse flakes of snow
Falling –
Touching my feeling
Which rises up to meet them.
My skin knows
They come from higher up
Higher than where I am now.
Something in my feeling part
Continues to rise up.
Looking, seeking
Unsure, unsatisfied.
Longing to be higher.
Then a wind comes
Turning what seemed like gentle flakes
Into needles on my skin.
Bringing me back to earth
To this planetary body that I inhabit.
Painfully I am aware
That the longing still is there.
Deep, unknown and inaccessible.
Humbly, I walk on.

A Golden Disk

A golden disk is shining before me
Inscribed with symbols
And quivering with life.
My mind wants to know.
It is hungry for meaning
But something says, "Feel."
I pause and wait,
Noticing an opening in my chest, in the region of my
heart.
An opening that allows the passage of light
A play of light.
And slowly I begin to understand
How that quivering disk of light
Is also here in me.
And in the reverberation between the two of us –
Meaning abounds –
The meaning of why I am here
For which there are no words.
No words but correspondences
That are perceived and tasted.
Something golden is embodied.
Golden and inscribed.

Dark

Dark.
A dark man
Rising up from muddy depths
Dripping black
Oozing black
Eyes closed.
Standing still
Dripping black
But emerged.
A step.
A small step.
Standing still again.
Dripping black.

A wind
A dry, cool wind.
The black begins to cake
And crack.
Another step.
Standing still again.
Instinctively
Taking a breath.
Standing still.
Still standing.
Taking a breath.

Day begins to break.
Eyes open to the light.
The black clay
Begins to crack and fall.
Bending down
Kneeling down
Forehead to the ground.
Thy will Lord, not mine.
Breathing.
Breathing still.
Still breathing.

The stars in Orion's belt
Are perfectly aligned.

Breathing.
Breathing still.
Still breathing.
Rise and stand again.
Stand tall.
Regard the turning firmament of stars.
Shine.
Shine on.
Without the dark, no stars.

Rejoice.

The Fool

Walking along the edge of a precipice
Carefree
And in a state of joy.
There is no discourse
No argument, rational and fine.
Walking forward
Not looking down
But looking up.
What is prayer?
It is a bell that rings
Announcing
Reconciling
Being more in tune
As we move from note to note.
I cannot and I can.
I know nothing and I know.
I am empty and I love.
Walking along the edge of a precipice.
Walking.
Alone.
And not alone.
The fool.

La Malinche

Al amanecer,
La montaña que se llama "La Malinche,"
O "Matlalcueye,"
Surge de la obscuridad de la noche,
Surge lentamente pero inexorable.

Esa montaña es como mi maestro
Me muestra algo que me falta –
Cómo ir hacia adelante,
Sin dudas, sin miedo, sin inquietud.
Lo que debo aprender –
¿Cómo proteger esto, de la mente?
Volviendo a mi cuerpo, porque él reconoce el alimento.
A través de los poros de mi piel, comienzo a comerme
la montaña.

La mente grita:
"¡No es posible comerse una montaña!"
"No." dice el cuerpo.
"Es posible. La comeré."
Lenta y inexorablemente, la como.
Siento su presencia en mi interior.
Siento su sabiduría y la agradezco.
¡Adelante!

Scouring

There is a surface
That I am responsible for.
This surface has been being polished
For longer than I am able to remember.
At first, it reflected almost nothing.
But with each scouring,
Bright patches began to appear,
Began to shine,
And reflect the light that was always there
From immemorial time.

When I look into this surface now
I see marching armies of the dead
Accompanied by the drums and tambours
Of delight and fright.
Clouds of dust are roiling in their wake.
They pass.
They come and go.
But always
After a time
Silence gathers into itself
The starry firmament above.
I look and look
As if there could never be enough looking
At what is above me.

Then, after a time,
I no longer look
Or see.
I find myself walking in darkness
Having forgotten this surface
I am responsible for.
I stop.
I remember.
Gradually I am aware of a distant glimmer
On the horizon.
I find patches
Where the scouring has not reached.

I am always finding those patches
And each time I am surprised
At their roughness and opacity.

I bring in grit and effort
Applied in earnest
And with love –
A love that was nurtured
Time and time again
From sources quite unknown
So that, for a time,
Once again,
I see and I am seen
In this surface
That I am responsible for.

Blessings be upon us now.

Prayer

"How could I not know what prayer is?"
Immediately, I ask:
"Who in me just said that?"
Followed by:
"What does it matter who?
What matters is that it was said.
And now
Where do I turn?"

Turn in the direction your feeling indicates
Adjust the frequency of your receptors
To the precise frequency
That is needed for communication to take place.

Stay.
Do not wait.
Stay.
You have a cosmic purpose.
Stay.
You are dust.
Stay.
Separate the fine from the coarse.
Stay.
Breathe.
Notice that something is received.
Something is deposited
Subtly
In precise inner places.
Stay.
Stay and rejoice.
I see and am seen.
I love and am loved.
My heart is larger now.
I am not alone.

Descent

I am told "down."
I am told "descent."
I am told "darkness."
Breathe in.
Breathe in the darkness.
It must enter fully into you.
Keep the jackals of the night at bay.
Their yelps must not deter your course.
Keep your gaze directed straight ahead
Even though you see nothing
Even though you are in darkness.
And realize now that you are larger.
You are vast.
Pinpoints of light appear in the darkness.
Dim at first, then stronger.
A firmament unfolds.
Sing.
Sing now of what you have become.
God needs this song.
Praise be.

Una nave azul

Veo una nave
Una nave azul
Flotando en el cielo.
Un diablito me dice, "¡Loco!".
Pero permanezco mirando
A mi nave azul en el cielo.
Continúo porque me siento mucho más tranquilo
Cuando estoy mirándola.

"¿Qué haces?" me pregunta mi diablito.

Hago un puente entre mi cuerpo
Y mi centro emocional.

"¡Loco!" repite mi amigo diablito.

Constato que mi nave tiene solamente
Dos asientos para pasajeros.
Una para mí; una para mi diablito.
Parece que nuestro destino
Es el de viajar juntos.

No estoy feliz.
El diablito tampoco.

Escuchamos a alguien reír en el cielo.

The Cauldron

There is a cauldron in the forest –
Three legs on its base
And its outside surface blackened from many fires.
Today it sits abandoned –
Titled at an angle
And wet from rain that falls unceasingly.
It was meant to contain something –
Something needing fire and transformation;
But it sits unused –
Abandoned to its memories.

"No."
"Not true," says a voice inside.
"This form is alive in you.
Watch.
See that it is now aligned
The tilt is gone
And a fire is kindled
In spite of the rain.

Place in the cauldron
What you must place in the cauldron.
Feed the fire.
Watch. Attend.
A transformation has begun.

This is what the mind is for.

Holding

Someone is holding a gemstone
At the center of my being.
It is facetted and clear
But its color is in constant movement.
How can this be?
Why have I not noticed this before?
The stone is held by a presence
Far beyond me
And yet distinct
Standing straight and tall.
I cannot see a face
But the uprightness
And the stillness speak to me
Richly
As if a certitude had descended into me
A certitude that has no words, no explanation
But is.
I am accompanied.
No longer am I alone.
And I shine.

Buttermilk and Cinnamon

Something is stirred
By the specificity of these tastes.
Just as an image can be a shining beacon,
Can these tastes evoke the illumination
Of undiscovered, inaccessible regions?
Confucius said, "Many can taste,
But few can distinguish the flavors."
Can I taste who I am?
Can I taste how you are?
Can I taste smoke in the fire of my longing to be?
The salt of a keenly felt remorse?
The cinnamon of inarticulate love?
A realm opens – unexplored, unsensed
But deliciously alive
Vibrating in harmony with
"All That Is."
Galaxies slip into me
And the laughter of the gods resounds
Through the buttermilk of transformation.
Holy, holy, holy is our wish to be.

10,000 Things

Rancid butter tea with salt.
Soot from the kettle ground into oily skin.
Growling trumpets rasping out their call.
An emerald lake, and shining peaks, and overarching
  blue.
The dwarf who limps and mumbles endlessly 10,000
  bitter things.

The path is empty now
And angels, wordless,
Sing.

Who is This?

In the kitchen sink
A yellow enamel basin
Full of warm soapy water.
Sunlight streaming down through the window,
Making the bubbles shine in rainbows.
Splashing – bubbles form and burst.
Cries of joy and laughter.
Spine straight.
Feeling water on the skin.
Feeling safe and protected.
Not a single care. Free in every way.

On horseback
Galloping across the Mongolian plain
Reins sticky with excitement
As we thunder forward.
Cries of joy and laughter
Rough laughter in the dusty sunlight
As women and children flee.
Not a single care. Free in every way.

A Line

Looking from this moment
I see a line of figures
Stretching back and forward in time –
A line that bears on this moment now;
A line borne by this moment.
I am in the moment but I feel the weight of that line.
I have felt this weight before
But only now in this moment
Do I feel the need to address
The members of this line.

The Mongolian horseman with his sword.
As I look into his eyes
His disdain is palpable
And yet a part of him is fearful
For he sees me as a ghost.
The realm of ghosts scares him
Binds him closer to his body and his sword.
Who and what is it that I cut down
In this life, in this moment?

One by one inviting them to this moment
So we can look into each other's eyes
So that we begin to know who we are.
Dying.
Dying again and again.
And not remembering.

Can I remember those members now?
As if each one adds a specific frequency to what is here
 and now.
Do I dare to invite each one?
The woman burned at the stake for healing.
The scholar of God angry at his body's animal life.
The Aztec Lord standing proud and sure

Resplendent in his feathered headdress.
Invite them all.

Moving on. Without hurry.
Steady on.
Who is it we must become?
The line stretching forward in time
Flickers.
Steady on.
I hear the angels sing.

Water

How can water be a cry,
Give voice,
Speak to me
Of who and what I am?
Water in all its forms:
The one I breathe;
The one I taste;
The one I slide across;
The water of which I'm made
Holding a charge
Emotional, electric
Infinitely adaptable
Able to be polluted
Or blessed.
Pointing to essence
Pointing to life.
I hear its laughter
Or its roar;
I hear its silence
And its age.
I am. We are.
Drink!

Unburdened

The river is far below
This winding road
Which is cut from living rock –
Rock that is orange and brown
And glistens
Here and there
With water.

We are stopped
By the movement of a hawk
And then find ourselves
Woven
Into the scene –
Made one, carried
On the same updraft,
And brought to rest
In the sunlight.

Far below, the river
Flows on
Unburdened by any
Heaviness of mind.

I See Now

I see now
That I am being spoken to
By all that lives.
The Canada goose
Standing by the shore in morning sunlight
Erect, listening.
I see how the listening
Manifests itself
In how she holds her neck.
This listening speaks to me.
And earlier this morning
Bending down
To examine the thin layer of frost
On every blade of grass,
Each blade knowing
That the sun will soon release
The burden of cold.
The knowing speaking to me now
So clearly.
And where do they fall in me
These messages, this silent language?
First a perception –
Then a part that stirs
Almost imperceptibly –
A quickening
The place of movement at the core –
An intimation
Of who and what I am
Of who and what we are.

THE EARTH SHUDDERS

The earth shudders –
A slight adjustment of plates
And then a single wave,
In seconds,
Turns neatly ordered Japanese lives
Into chaos and debris.

A priest has come to stand
Erect and unshakeable
Amid the devastation.
Snow falls gently over all.
And one hand holds a bell with which to call.

He is a pillar between worlds –
The world of those departed lives,
And this world of broken dreams.
Nothing shakes his gaze or his intent.
His chant is audible and deep.
Calling, calling out to what is gone
But still lives on –
Departed souls
Who doubtless listen now
With unperturbed intent
Freed from earthly bonds.

And not so far away
The ocean murmurs still.

A Timeless Time

I could not see the gesture
But a gesture there must have been.
What else could have drawn me
Under the gentle protection of that tree
At the corner of 72nd and Lex?
Although it was not yet 10 in the morning
And the day was overcast still,
My mind reasoned that it would be cooler there
As I waited for the traffic light to change.
But once there, something became engaged –
A communication:
How he was proud
Of the fullness he had become;
How he stood for something;
How he worked, yeoman-like,
For the spreading of an influence –
And it mattered not
That these skittish humans paid no heed.
He was proud nonetheless
Because he knew – beyond all doubt –
That he flourished so
Because of the gaze from Above
Within which he had his life
And song.
In my body I could feel
The movement of this conversation –
How a quiver of delight
Was there at each of the affirmations he conveyed.
But also the precision of the feeling
Transmitted somehow out of me
Like an arm around his shoulder
Or a smile flashed in the eyes,
Just as in any heartfelt encounter
There is the point and counterpoint
Of feeling elements exchanged.

Time opened for us
In the time it takes
For a traffic light to change.

Bluestone

(For Hy and Rosanne)

It was an old bluestone quarry
Now abandoned, he explained.
Perhaps they had hit a spring
And it had filled with water to make this pond.

Reflected in the still surface
The sheered-off rock face was blue, yes
A blue-grey slate,
But tinged with a soft orange in places too –
A delicate interweaving of color
In the fading evening light.

The willow he had planted was now full grown,
Its presence integral to what was suspended there,
To what hung in the air.

The slope of the land leading down to the water's edge,
The standing grove of evergreens all along the top of
the rock face.
A clear day in June, but cool.
Wispy clouds high above
And the purple martins' house on its pole.

As if another mouth and throat
Opened
To drink in
What was suspended there –
Something that proceeded invisibly,
Interpenetrating through each element
On which the vision came to rest.

Such rest.

And more mysterious still – the movement inside
Of something fed.

Only later seeing
That what was suspended there –
What was sensed and what was felt –
Could not be said.

The Voice of the Earth

The voice of the earth
Rising up through my feet and into me.
The vibration is ongoing
Centered low down in the body
Speaking of the taste
Of chill autumn air and
The waxing and waning pull of the moon.
Not a complaint
But a low murmur of life
On a planetary scale.
Gradually a kinship is felt –
A recognition spreads.
Yes. I am of the earth.
I sojourn here.
I too feel the pull of the moon
And the chill of autumn air.
The scale is vast.
Not just the moon but the stars as well
Touch some barely remembered part
Close, very close
To the heart.
Listen!
Hers is the voice of love.

Seven White Lilies

Seven white lilies have risen
Amid the rubble where a house once stood.
One wall, red brick, still and quiet.
No roof.
All is open to the sky.
And these lilies have a song
An endless song
That rarely can be heard.
It is a song of joy
Joy and adoration.
Sunlight pours down
Starlight pours down
Moonlight pours down
Rain and shine
But forever this song goes on.
Hallelujah
Glory Hallelujah.

Life after Death

He said we must –
Before we die –
Have done all we can
To have an image or a concept
Of life after death.
The critical mind revolts
And says, "Ridiculous. Impossible."
But this morning, in early sunlight,
As I walked through a grove of pines near the lake
I was struck by a stillness
And I stopped.
The presence of these stately pines
Brought a hush to the moment.
Their life, their reaching up
Was palpable.
Not only palpable,
It was as if a wordless communication was engaged –
A recognition – here is life –
A mutual recognition
And a smile.
Dead twigs and needles were a smooth carpet for
    my feet –
Death and life side by side.
My concept then of life after death
Is that I will be met
Just as today I was met
By these trees
And I will be accompanied
As I continue to move on and on
In another life
A life that is the same and not the same.

The Raven

First the voice, the gravelly voice
Coming from the redwood forest.
Insistent, deep.
And then the enormous sweep of wings
Dark wings
Soaring to the ground
Out of sight
But not out of mind.
Even now, in this present moment,
Hours later,
Something is stirred
By that voice
By those dark wings
An informing that continues on.
What does that dark wing and gravelly voice
Touch in me?
Clearly something very specific is touched
Right there, just there.
There is no word
There are no words
For that movement deep within
A call to come to Earth
But not to be Earth-bound.
A call to know that, to be that.
Bless you raven
For the gift of who you are.

Blue

I am accompanied by someone blue.
At first it seemed a little strange
But now there is a feeling of friendship
Or at least a feeling of something shared –
Like a summer smile exchanged.
It reminds me of a sapphire I once saw –
A sizable jewel stone
That drew me in as I looked into its depths.
It's like that in feeling
But also not like that in reality
Since my new friend is invisible.
I do not see, I feel, the blueness.
And how to speak about the communication that
we have . . .
This wordless communication
Like the dialogue between the brilliantly white
Blossoms of the pear
And the wind.
A movement, a participation.
Being together.
No longer alone.
Living a kind of fullness
That is unfamiliar in this incarnation
But eminently alive.
And timeless.
Worlds.
Worlds within worlds.
I am blue.

Taking Flight

I have a friend now,
A serpent friend,
Who is asking me to give him power.
I must confess
That I have been reluctant
To be seen with him
In public.
Shameful behavior on my part really.
After all, it was I
Who asked to be his friend.
And he accepted with a smile.
A quiet smile
Deep and mysterious
Reflecting the depth of wisdom
He embodies.
A millennial wisdom born of dark earth
And sun and sky.
His blue skin glistens in the light
As he moves
From one place to the next.
Always close.
Always by my side.
Always accompanying me.

He is teaching me to fly.
No ordinary serpent this.
His wings are plumed
In orange and yellow –
The color of fire.
Together we rise up,
Effortlessly take flight,
Soaring in the midnight sky –
Midnight blue
Reverberating

In a quiet tone.
He turns to me now,
Looks me in the eye
And says, "Thank you
For giving me the power I desire.
Our hearts now beat as one.

And our journey of friendship
Has begun.
May the learning we garner
Each from each
Never find its end."

PHOTO: Anne Évangéline LeBlanc.
TATTOO: Guillaume, Montreal www.gustattoo.ca

Quetzalcoatl

A barely audible hiss attracts my attention.
It takes me a while to realize
That Quetzalcoatl has something to say to me.
His blue skin reflects the light in a myriad of waves.
As he moves toward me,
His orange and yellow plumes quiver and sway.
Then motionless he holds me in his gaze.
"What is it that I have forgotten to ask?" I say.
"You have forgotten to ask how you will live long
enough
Before you pass," he replies.
"Ah, yes, I have often wondered about that," I say.
"But wondering is such a flabby response," he retorts.
"You need to know."
"And how can I know? Tell me how. I ask this of you
now with great respect."
"You know the answer of course and have known it for
some time. But you do not engage with what you
know. The process is simple – you must shed your
skin. There is a new one underneath."
"But I don't know how to shed my skin," I said. "I am
not like you for whom that comes naturally."
"Not so. You are more like me than you care to admit,"
he says with an inner, very visible, smile.
"It's very simple. It depends only on a recognition – a
recognition of what is dead. Once you see what is
dead, and you know clearly that it is dead, it will move
out to the skin and be shed. That is what your skin is
for. You have this capacity. It's just that you don't use
your God-given faculties as they were designed to be
used – so intelligently designed, by the way. With this
clear seeing you will live exactly as long as you need to
live. And then you will pass. It's so simple really. This
is an important element of your work now. Do not
forget. And if you do I will remind you."

"I am so glad we will live this together you and I,"
I said.
"And I am glad as well my friend," he whispered as he
took his leave.

Q Prime

My friend the plumed serpent
Is speaking to me now
But not in words.
He smiles, he looks
Into my eyes
And something is exchanged.
"Forget the words."
For a while those words flash
Before me like a neon sign.
And then they fade away.
It is quiet.
Still I hold his gaze
Lightly
Not fixedly.
Gently there is a stirring
And a movement of feeling.
I turn to the right and see unfolding
A vista of stars and planets
Stretching off into an infinite distance.
Turning back I catch a twinkle in his eye.
Softly he whispers,
"Remember."

The Elixir

The dragon smiled
As he observed the antics of the human in his charge.
Heaving a heart-felt sigh
Half to himself, he muttered,
"Well, at least now he has glimpsed me several times.
But his attention flickers so –
Will he ever hold his vision clear?"
Sunlight glints along his scales
As he undulates his way through cloud and storm
Through night and day.
"The age is ending now," he musingly remarks.
"Time is running fast.
Let's inject him with the thought that he can ride.
He hears!
My goodness, he actually hears me now.
But wait, his brain engages.
Maybe thought was not enough.
But oh, yes, the elixir.
Quickly. Just one dose will do.
Excellent. His eyes are brighter now.
His vision clears.
The sensation of his heels digging into my back
Holds him firm."

Laughing now
We fly.

The Emerald

How to come to rest inside
With what I have been given?
This gift of an emerald
Is before me now
Its depths unplumbed.
I look and look
Until finally it is clear
That I am not looking with my heart.
Engage.
Feel.
Enter in.
The eyes of the serpent are green
And deep.

"Be very still," he whispers to me now.
"Come with me down these stairs
Come with me to the cavern below ground
My lair.
Here we commune with green
Here we commune with heart
And we are one.
There is a storehouse of knowledge here.
You know and you are known.
Enter deeply in."

Gradually I begin to hear the shaman's song
The crystal clarity of tone
Carrying me
Carrying me
Until, until
The end
Where I am sitting once again
Looking at a stone.

Three in One

On my right, a serpent of great beauty
And great danger.
"Copperhead they call me," was his hissed reply
To my querulous look.

And on my left, a mouse.
Grey and timorous
Shaking through every sinew of his frame.

I lay my magic wand between them
And the evident strain immediately is gone.

Good.
Now we can talk.

Snake tell me, how can I love you?
In the past I fled from you
But now, your appearance here
In this magic land
Tells me I need you.

"First, drop your fear.
Second, look carefully at my skin.
As you stare at the patterns of copper and of gold
You will enter into relationship with me.
Do you feel that slight movement in your belly?"

"Yes, I do."

"Good. Stay with that movement
And you will find that I am an indispensable part
Of who you are."

"Yes, it is so!"

"When are you going to release to me
My lunch sitting on your left?"

"That is not your lunch.
That is your ally.
And mine."

"You must be mad. That is my lunch."

"You must now learn from me
As I have learned from you.
Your life depends upon the mouse."

"Ridiculous," is the hissed reply.
"He offers nothing to either you or me."

"Not so! He offers his timidity, his grey-ness.
He offers us who he is.
Softness can be lovely."

Hissing softly the snake
Turns his gaze to the mountain vista behind me.

Just then, a beating of wings is heard
But nothing is seen.
All three of us very alert
As we feel that light is descending all around us.
Stillness enters.
The place is numinous.
A powerful voice is heard:

"Your wand of separation is critical.
Use it well.
With time all three are one."

A White Horse

A white horse
Stamping his feet and whinnying.
Smiling at me.
Laughing at me.
"What took you so long?
I have been waiting for you here for ages!"
"Me on a white horse!" I say.
"How could that be? I've never ridden a horse!"
"No one is asking you to agree," he says.
"No one except your destiny of course."
"My destiny? I was told no one has a destiny."
"And you believed them?
The time is now. The stirrups and the reins await you."

Without a leap, I am there.
Feet secure in the stirrups.
Reins lightly held in the hands.
We are as one. Merged.
Great power and suddenly also – wings.
We fly.

"Do not look back," he says.
"Only look forward – and you will be fine.
Keep your heart vigilant and strong.
We approach the Pleiades now."

I smile a quiet smile.

Touch

Something came
But it was not a word
It was a touch – the touch of a wing
On my back –
Unmistakable
But immeasurably light
And overflowing with significance
With meaning –
Simply true.

In that eternal instant
Knowing unconditionally
That I am with . . .
With that . . .
Regardless of how far
I may have wandered
Or how far I may have distanced myself
No matter –
I am
Loved.

Glory

Glory
Is the formless robe
She wears
Proceeding toward us
Silently
From the realm of light that yet will be.
Beneficent is her look,
Potent, her gaze
And glory is also streaming now
In unimpeded song –
Holy, Holy, Holy
On wings most high.

Un mouvement

Il y a un mouvement dans ces mots :
« Seigneur ayez pitié ».
Un mouvement qui me transperce ;
Un mouvement qui résonne dans tout mon corps.
J'étends mon bras
Et la résonnance est là.
Tout le long du bras un son
Qui rend le bras plus léger –
Mon bras est soulevé, soutenu, activé.
Dans la tête un silence profond –
Pas d'associations –
Comme si le silence permettait le mouvement
De ces mots dans mon corps.
Graduellement, je deviens conscient de mon cœur,
De cette partie si souvent abandonnée
Qui maintenant fait partie du tout.
Il y a un mouvement là aussi,
Un mouvement que je distingue à peine.
Je n'ai pas de nom pour ce mouvement,
Tellement il m'est inconnu.
Mais quelque chose est claire –
Je participe à un mouvement.
Je ne suis plus mort.
Seigneur ayez pitié.

Archangel Uriel

Archangel Uriel
Holds a sword in his right hand
And a flame in his left hand.
His face is delicate but stern.
The sword is pointing up, vertical;
The flame is love.
I ask him for help.
I ask, "How can I love my fellow man?"
And he replies, "Fear not."
I ask him to help my hobbled feet.
They do not take me where I need to go.
The sword glints.
I do not see it move
And my feet are freer now.
But still I do not know, I do not move.
There is a barely perceptible smile
And he says, "Once you have moved, you will ask
again.
I will be here.
Always.
Know that you are accompanied.
Know that you are loved."

She Came Riding

She came riding on a great white horse
With laugher and with joy
Wind in her hair and in the horse's mane.
Jumping lightly down and holding tightly to the reins
She strode to where I stood and said,
"Have no fear.
Just as the wind has carried me here
In laughter and in joy
So will it carry you as well.
You need only mount and ride.
The wind is all you need.
And its will is not of your concern.
Just sound the bell,
Call it and it will come.
Fear not."
For a moment more
She stood before me still
Eyes closed,
Listening, listening hard and fast.
And then with a final smile
She turned and soon was gone
Leaving behind her now
Only the wind
And me.

What the Eagles Said

The space between –
Between planets in one or another star system –
The arc of that, the arch of that, the canopy of that
Moving down, down and down
Down into a movement in the chest
Infinitely fine
Slight vertigo when faced with this immensity
Listen, listen, listen hard and fast
We speak to you
We are between
Between the branches
Between the interstices of thought
Between the blue threads of time
We speak to you because you are needed
You all are needed
We all are needed
We are
And in our are-ness there is a flow.
Reach out.
Reach out and touch this flow.
Feel its texture.
Taste, savor its elemental nature.
Be in this larger world.
The choice is yours.
We await you.
This current awaits you.
Consciousness awaits you.
Be.

Still

He did not appear
    But he was there.
He had no form
    But he was there.
Without substance
    But substantial.
He took no space
    But he was there.
He said nothing
    But I was instructed.
He did nothing
    But knots were untied.
He made no gesture
    But I was touched.
We did not move
    But I was accompanied.
No time passed
    But he was there.
Now he is not
    And yet he is.
Time has passed
    And no time has passed.
My heart is opening still.

You

How to say what it is you bring? –
When you come to me like this
Unexpected.
I drift, I feel rudderless, I feel assailed
And then
You are with me.
No time has passed.
No time can pass.
No time.
Now I feel deeply rooted, unassailable
And yet mobile.
There is a lightness and yet care and precision
In each movement I make.
And, ah, how to say what is in the heart?
There is boundlessness
And yet I am not burdened or flooded.
I am more.
More of who I could be.
I am assured of that.
Neither sweet nor bitter.
A boundless embrace
In which I am held.
For no gain.
For no end.
For ever.

The Gyre

Watching the muses dance,
Hearing their song
Weaves me in
While extracting me
From enchantment
With the thick and the dark.
Now I feel the stars.
Their fingers press lightly
Down into me.
Here and here and here.
My breathing too
Reaches further and further.
The spine lengthens
And its serpent laughs.
Ankles flex
And the liver clears its throat.
I sing the silent wordless song
Of my interstellar life.
The gyre expands
And I am carried
Home.

Skrying 2

He was given the gift of skrying
That ancient art of looking into a reflective surface
In order to glimpse
What normally remains unseen.
At first he saw very little –
Shadowy outlines
But movement nonetheless.
With time and practice
There was more clarity and definition.
Then there was travel to distant worlds.
There were meetings with the dead.
And then there were things that could not be said.
But what was he to do with these seeings?
No one else saw them.
He asked for the gift to be returned
But that was not possible
Because now the seeing came
Whether or not there was a reflective surface.
What was he to do?
He asked for an intervention
From the source of the original gift.
But the response was not what he had asked for.
"Travel on, my son," said the voice.
"This is your journey now and you must find your way.
You have come this far.
Do not falter. Fear not.
You are not alone.
Look to your heart. Feel your way.
And listen to your song."

Sophia

She came riding,
Riding in a chariot of gold,
Her hair the color of burnished copper
Undulating in the air behind her.
Through clouds of fire
Flaming with the light of dawn she rode.
Her gaze was fixed intently on some distant goal
And lightly there rested in her hands
The blue-tinged reins
As her four white horses galloped on.

Below her path the city slept
Unaware of what was passing through the skies above.
Except perhaps for one or two who felt in a curious way
That something moved above them
And perhaps they wondered how they were to be
With what passed so indistinctly through their inner
realms.
Could room be made for that fiery passage
That was so far above them
Yet so close.
So close and so present in an inner world
Outside of time and space?

And what trembles in anticipation of their possible
success?

The Orb

The orb I was given could not be touched
Because it belonged to another world
And yet it shone with a warm and steady light.
Why was I given such a thing
If it really could not be mine?
"And what then is mine?" I heard myself say.
"What is there that is not just on loan?"
"Is anything mine?"
The orb continued to shine with its warm and steady
light
Through all these questionings.

I see the heron float across the lake and land.
An oh so graceful approach and touching down.
What am I being shown?
Where do I touch down?
The planet supports me and gives me life
But I belong to another world
A world of light.
Can I breathe in two worlds at the same time?
The orb comes closer now
There is a gentle pulsation in its light.
I feel supported
Supported in my heart.
Gratitude washes over me
For what I have received.
Is there anything that is not a gift?

Dialogue with Uriel

Jack: My heart does not know where to turn. As if it missed being educated. What can be done about this?
Uriel: You need to make more mistakes.
Jack: That sounds very painful.
Uriel: The heart cannot be educated without pain.
Jack: But I don't want to be hurt.
Uriel: You see that in my right hand I carry a sword and in my left a heart. Consider that carefully.
Jack: I'm not sure I understand you.
Uriel: Ask your heart.
Jack: My heart says it understands perfectly.
Uriel: So perhaps now your head understands that the education needs to take place in the heart not in the head.
Jack: Yes, but I wonder where my heart will find its strength.
Uriel: Ask the sunrise.
Jack: And what about love? It is a great mystery to me.
Uriel: Consider the night sky on a clear night. Feel its overarching embrace. Start there and then go on from there.
Jack: Go on to where?
Uriel: You will find the way.
Jack: I love our conversations Uriel.
Uriel: So do I Jack.

El Águila

Veo el águila
Que se posa en el alto pino.
Me dice:
"Bienvenido al país de las aves.
Quiero decirte
Una cosa importante:
Aprender a volar
Es un talento crucial."

¡Pero no soy ave!
"No importa.
Puedes aprender.
Ten confianza.
Te ayudaré.
Juntos volamos.
Ahora, en este momento . . .
Está muy bien volar sobre las montañas, ¿verdad?"
Sí. ¡Es maravilloso!

"¿Y puedes ver cómo una parte en tu interior es cambiada?"
Sí. Me siento más ligero.
"¿Y puedes ver cómo es útil?"
Sí, claro.

Forget the Bridge

This morning I came across a bridge.
The word "bridge" reverberates,
Touches deep inside
And something begins to weep.
One more bridge
But not the bridge my heart desires.
And yet . . .
And yet . . .

I stop.
I smile.
Poor old me.

Stillness resumes.

An eagle with a white pigeon in its claws
Lands near me.
His eyes are sharp and fearless.
"Forget the bridge," he says.
"Fly. Fly until you see the stars.
Orion's belt is yours
The Pleiades – the seven sisters – are your family.
The overarching arms of heaven welcome you in.
Take a breath and fly."

And so
I do.
The bridge is formless
And so am I.

I am.

Just This

Who is this figure I see walking?
A figure clothed in light and dark
Walking, walking on.
I cannot see the face
Because I am looking from behind.
But there is something in the stride
Something free and unrestrained
A steady movement forward
Neither forceful nor forced.

A shock.
A shock somewhere in the chest
As I realize that this figure
Is moving forward
Towards a star.
The name of the star is Sirius.
Sirius rising now
Just above the horizon
Crystal clear
In the dry cool desert air.
This figure
And this stride
Moving forward
Steadily.
A whiff of cinnamon and jasmine
Enters
Circulates
And I realize that I am born.
Born of this.
Just this.

Sacred fire

There is a sacred fire that burns unnoticed in the hearts
of men.
It smolders until the day when a dark curtain is burnt
through
Allowing the light of heaven to pour down into the
depths where feeling dwells unborn.
Now the man with feeling born is once again a child,
His right hand reaching heavenward, feeling for a hand
to clasp.
And how to say, as the two hands touch, what then
transpires in the hearts of men with feeling born?
No need to say, but only feel that there is neither man
nor God
But only love.

Petrified

For M'Lou
With Thanks

Head thrown back,
Hips and genitals tucked under,
Every muscle held,
Wrenched against the fear –
Fear so great there is no scream.
There is no breath to scream.
A body turned to stone.
Darkness is drawn down
Drawn all around
So that nothing enters the boundaries
Of a self enclosed.

I take up this body,
This small body,
The body of a child of three or four,
A body rigid and cold,
Wrapping it warmly
In a cashmere blanket of midnight blue.
And I lay this agonizing form
Against me
On the heart side of my chest.
And I wait.
And I breathe.
And I open my heart to love.

Over days
The form begins to melt
Against me.
Abandoned for 75 years
The stone now begins to shake
And turn to tears,
Shaking and tears,
As I hold him closer
And begin to rock him gently

Into song.

More days pass
Until one day
We sit together
Laughing at the sun.

The Blue Mist of Timelessness

Surrounded by the blue mist of timelessness,
I move forward.
I see nothing but the mist.
And yet I must move forward.
Fear or discouragement must not be
Allowed to dwell in the heart.
Their entry, it seems, I cannot prevent
But they must not dwell there.
Nor can they dwell in my feet.
Step by step
Each toe adapts to the unevenness
Of the path I cannot see.
Each toe singularly and in concert with the others.
Big breath in.
I hear myself saying,
"I cannot see and I walk alone."
Very softly I also hear,
As if from very far,
"Are you sure?"
And suddenly I become aware
That although I cannot see
I nevertheless can feel
That I am not alone.
Nothing further needs be said
Nor needs to be
As I continue to move forward
Step by step.
In the blue mist of timelessness.

TONES OF THE HEART

Master Kung, it is said,
Spoke of the inarticulate tones of the heart.
Listen.
Do not speak.
Listen.
And I hear a tumbling jungle of tones.
Nothing articulate.
Where does the syntax of articulation reside?
A faculty that seems unknown, unplumbed.
I am searching for the tone of acceptance.
Because of unwelcome circumstances
It is urgent that I articulate this tone
And that I articulate it now.
Instinctively I take a deep breath
And I sense a small movement stirring
At the base of the skull.
Suddenly I am aware that I am standing in front of
    something,
Something close up, not far from my face.
Again a deep breath.
I am breathing in what is in front of me
But what is in front of me
Is in no way reduced.
A presence grows.
A presence in the heart.
Acceptance is there.
It is alive there.
And now I breathe.
I breathe more freely.
I am articulate.

PHOTO: Michel Zabé

Attended Snowball, Ontario (Canada) Public School: a one-room, red brick building with a pot-bellied wood stove for heat in the winter. Did university. Learned French. Wrote haiku for a while. Enjoyed a stimulating career in library automation including repeated visits to clients in Japan, Taiwan and Korea. Dabbled in linguistics. Helped computerize the Inuit language, Inuktitut.

At retirement age began using altered states of consciousness (still misnamed hypnosis) and an energy modality called Reconnective Healing™ to help seekers with their journey through terrestrial life. (www.trylus.com)

Fell in love with Mexico. Learned some Spanish.

Continue to be itinerant.

Comment Received

When I began the project of collecting some of my writing for possible publication I had some concern about whether or not others could really engage with what I had written. However, I was encouraged warmly by even the first few friends I shared it with. But what struck me most strongly was the following comment I received. It is so strong that I felt it deserved its own place in the book. Its author not wishing to be named, perhaps I could just say it was penned by a friend from another planet – as the diction makes clear.

"About the works: They do speak of a certain beauty of life that is dear to me, I think to all, deep within. It needs to be treasured and at the same time let go. It is a language closer to me than English despite it being (mostly) in English. I could say it is written in my language, in terms of how I too perceive and construct my notions of reality. It brought me to tears a few times for personal reasons such as missing my friends who speak in this language and seeing some of them, including myself, fall prey to business English and other for-profit manipulations necessary for daily life but then assimilated beyond return."

"From my notes: These are universal, experiential, practical (in the sense of actual help one can use by participating in their ongoing transmission) journeys of the fabric (a thread throughout: being seen and not being alone) of shared experience. They are connected, therefore aspects of the truth, by which they are timeless and accessible. "Being seen" and a togetherness of atmospheres and life on various parallel ongoing realms visible and invisible by the faculties of life on all those levels. Redefining the boundary-lessness of aloneness. You mention it is part of individual work in/within a group setting. I think that is unique. The content is not made up or "imaginary" as much of today's poetry but imaginal. Although imagination probably plays that entrancing role of a point of initialization."